A Suitcase and a Dream
My True Story
From Foster to Prosper

D1547678

Brittney Sherell

MANIFOLD GRACE
Publishing House LLC

A Suitcase and a Dream: My True Story from Foster to
Prosper
Copyright © 2018 Brittney Sherell

Cover Design: CreativeLogoArt

All scriptures taken from King James Version of the Holy
Bible.

ISBN: 978.1.937400.07.1

Printed in the United States of America

Published by Manifold Grace Publishing House, LLC
Southfield, Michigan 48033
www.manifoldgracepublishinghouse.com

Dedications

In Loving Memory
Of
My Paw Paw
Kertrece V. Florence
Falon D. Noble
Apostle William T. Nichols
Truck Driving "Chef" Mike Johnson
My favorite Auntie Doris Minott
Granny (Grace)

Acknowledgments

To my Lord and Savior, the one who made all of this possible, thank you for saving me, and allowing me to be here to write this book. I now know where my strength comes from.

Thank you for allowing me to minister, to share my story with your people. Lord, I love you so very much. You deserve all of the praise, the glory and the honor. All I wanted to do was tell my story and help heal people; one story at a time and one poem at a time.

To the therapist at The Children's Home of Detroit who helped make this possible. When I sat in the office and said "I want to write a book", they handed me a pamphlet. They are one of the reasons you are reading this today.

Evangelist Debra McNair, you are the main reason I was able to leave Michigan and start my life in Georgia, I love you!

Apostle Veter Nichols, my foundation, you are the reason I know God and have a relationship with him. Thank you! Because of you, I still attend church today.

Ms. Teal, thank you so much from the bottom of my heart.

Foster Parents: Terry Griffin, Karen and Bobby Brisby and Jean Ginzel. I love you all so much. I would not be who I am today without having known you.

My sisters: I'm thankful for the relationship that we have. I love you all.

Donita Frazier, Myckelle Williams, Tony Robinson, Stephanie Brabson, Pearl Ramsey, S.O.N.S, Angela Shenell, Eboni Johnson, Collen Nxumalo, Ms. Rita, Michelle Scott Thomas, Cherish Fields, Judge Penny Brown Reynolds, Fanci Lewis, JHill, Alaska Airlines, Dionne Smith Christopher, Colette Lovelady, LaWanda Moody, LeeVon Murdock, Terri VanDorn, Ms. Star, Mrs. Tiffany Wood, Essie Bryan, TLC, Schaffer.

My one and only brother: I love you!

My biological father: I love you!

Kathy, my biological mother: I forgive you, and I love you!

The Brown Family: Barbara, Kevin and Martine, we may not talk every day but you all keep me grounded. Meeting you guys was one of the best things to ever happen to me.

Social Workers: Naomi Page-Baba, Heather Marie Robinson Moore, Michelle Jackson, Chiquita Ford-White, you all mean the absolute most to me. Some of the best social workers in the State of Michigan.

Thank you all so much!

TABLE OF CONTENTS

Foreword

Brittney S. Turner loved, loved, loved a show I starred in on the Nickelodeon network, The Kenan & Kel Show! She sent me an email introducing herself and letting me know she was a huge fan. It was something about Brittney that resonated with me and separated her from any other "fan". It's what prompted me to personally reach out and call Brittney. Her voice, her story, her truth was profound and our connection was instant; as well as effortless.

When Brittney openly shared her foster care life with me, I listened intently because what Britt did not know at the time was, I had served as a CASA (Court Appointed Special Advocate for youth at risk) and unfortunately, her story was familiar to me. Her hustle & flow life. But what I most admired about Brittney, then as I do now, is her willingness to be real and raw. Her words that trace her journey from youth to present, as a young adult, are simply mind blowing. Every time I turned a page or scanned a chapter, I became more in awe of a person who has truly endured hardships that could have closed chapters and left blank pages a long time ago. And yet Brittney Sherell Turner is here. From the secret girlfriend, promiscuity, and suicide attempts by way of a rubbing alcohol concoction, Brittney, at 13, began putting her pen to paper with *A Suitcase and a Dream* as she states, for her internal survival.

For anyone in or out of trauma, to be able to articulate a perfectly imperfect life of rape, neglect, homelessness, mental illness and much more, so early in life, exemplifies a bravery, a grit, a determination for a spirit to free itself like never before and hopefully to free the readers.

Through her authentic self, I too am reminded that the need to be a positive force in someone's life is truly a necessary "thing". It's not about coming and going as one pleases, though one pleases to do so. We must actually pause and pay attention and strive for no missed opportunities. The question is, to those of us who genuinely can: Will you answer the call?

To write this foreword, from one Michigan girl to another, is my honor and gratefully I answered the call from Brittney as it has reminded us both to not let a barrier block a destiny!

Brittney's reality, I believe, will have you as a possible difference maker, sit back and think, maybe I really am my brother's keeper, maybe I can and should stand, be heard, be courageous, be tenacious, be intentional, be the one who walks in the wilderness with the downtrodden, the abused, the misguided and, be the change!

To the one who has lived, or is living, a parallel life as told by Brittney, I trust her story will give you a liberation that you may have thought was impossible. But then it is through her voice of sheer determination and hope that you can realize your freedom is possible and that you and your words matter. You are not alone!

The past can fuel you as it did for Brittney, so fill up! Read and be encouraged. Don't forget to pack only what you need to positively feed your soul!

Teal Marchande,

Intro

"When my heart is overwhelmed lead me to the rock that is greater than I."

Psalm 61:2, one of my favorite scriptures. I remember Mrs. Sharon Francois teaching me this scripture so I actually know this one by heart. It really helped when I almost lost my life back in 2017. But that's another book.

"I am Brittney. I am poetry. I am the dark-skinned girl you talked about in school. I am the annoying little girl that lived across the street. I am being me. I am the reason nobody can flow like me, simply because you know nothing about me. I am poetry!"

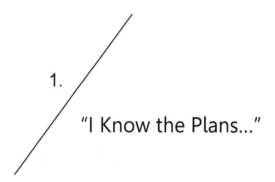

1.

"I Know the Plans..."

My sister and I were born on March 24, 1992 in Flint, Michigan at St. Joseph Hospital. Bianca and I were born to Katharine Winona Stanford at 6:02p.m. and 6:04p.m., respectively. Momma had a total of 5 children; 4 girls and 1 boy - Eddie Wayne Jr. Bianca, Brittney, Brandi and Baejanae (Bae-ja-nae), we did not grow up with our brother.

I do not recall my dad being in my life unless it was on a weekend, then he would come and pick us up. That was it, other than that we never saw him. I'm ok with that now. It bothered me then that I did not see him as much as I would have liked to. But hey, you can't make someone be a father. I remember my cousin

Rose. She would pick us up quite often and we would go shopping, or to some type of amusement park. Like Cedar Pointe in Ohio, or Chuckie Cheese. Rose was my favorite cousin.

If I did not have anyone else, I had my Granny. She was my world, she was my rock. I loved her to life. We did everything together, she and I used to get up early in the morning and go grocery shopping, then I would go with her to get her hair done and run other errands. And when we were done, we would walk in the house and yell "I'm back" and everybody would come running upstairs.

We had to be in bed at 8:00 p.m. so at 7:59 p.m., I'd run all the way upstairs from the basement to my Granny. And I would get in the bed with her. I would be on her left side, reading the newspaper and looking at "In the Heat of the Night", Granny's favorite show. Just being in the bed with her, made me feel like the richest little girl in the world. She would have 2 pieces of butterscotch candy on her nightstand, waiting for me. I had never felt love the way my Granny loved me. It didn't even matter that my mom was on drugs, because Granny had everything under control. I'd lie in bed with her until I fell asleep, and loved every moment with her, even the perfume she wore. I wish I knew the scent.

I grew up on 510 West Hamilton St., Northside. Flint, MI. I always loved it when Granny cooked, especially her desserts. She used to make these brownies with walnuts and raisins, or she would make a peach cobbler. Granny would leave the brownies on the counter, wrapped up. My sisters and I would sneak downstairs in the middle of the night just to have another taste of what heaven tasted like. Her brownies would just melt in your mouth.

Granny was the sweetest person I knew. But she didn't play! I can remember playing in the garage and we broke something. She came out and asked "Who did it?" I pointed to my sister so fast. She took that whipping for me. I don't remember what we did the next time, but I remember the whipping like it was yesterday. My sister and I were taking a bath and it was time to get out. Granny came in with a switch, we got our butts TORE UP. You can bet we slept well that night.

We were only allowed in the living room and dining room on holidays, and Granny kept plastic on the couch. I can remember sneaking in the living room to watch The Cosby Show, and if I heard my Granny coming, I'd slip out the double doors leading to the hallway.

We spent a lot of time playing outside. We were never allowed to play in the front yard and we'd better not get near Granny's flower bed. It started at the end of the driveway and ran all the way up to the garage. Playing hide and seek in the basement – who remembers those big furnaces that made the loud noises? Bianca and I were hiding behind it, and I kept pushing her back. The next thing you know, Bianca got burned. Granny comforted her, and nursed her, and fixed her up. Granny was a nurse.

Let me tell you, the first time we ever had hot sauce, we had gone to KFC and put hot sauce all over our chicken. Honey, let me tell you, our butts were on fire! But once again, Granny was there to save the day. She laid each of us across her legs and put Vaseline on our burning behinds. No matter the situation, Granny was there to save the day. Whether we lived up the street or around the corner, I never wanted to leave my Granny. I wanted to live with her. But I never could.

She used to send us to the store for her beer. She drank "Big Bear". Sometimes momma would send us to Granny's house for food. We would ride our bikes and have bags of meat hanging on the handle bars. I'm getting emotional just thinking about her. You walk in her house and you smelled food. It was just a sweet aroma, whatever was on the stove, you automatically knew it was going to be good.

There was always a sweet spirit in her house. I absolutely loved mornings with Granny. I never knew what would await me when I got to the kitchen table in the corner next to the small TV on the counter. We had hot breakfast every single morning. Honey, my Granny did not miss a beat; whether it was cream of wheat with wheat toast and apple butter, or oatmeal with apples and raisin toast. Granny made sure her grandbabies were set. And at 8:15 a.m., we walked out the door and headed to school, cutting between the neighbor's house where we met our favorite crossing guard. Granny always sent a Christmas gift for her, and the crossing guard would do the same for Granny.

We had a neighbor, Ms. Louie, and whenever we had loose teeth, she would tie string to the tooth that was loose, and attach it to the door knob, then pull out the tooth. Afterwards, she gave us Superman ice cream on a cone. That was the best ice cream in the world, and still is. It wasn't a birthday party if there was no Superman ice cream.

Then we had Bob and Liz, an older white couple that lived in a black and white house. Mrs. Liz used to make gingersnap cookies and give them to us in the backyard over the fence. They were some nasty cookies, but we ate them!

If you ask me, Granny had the cutest house on the block. It was a brick house with a fence around the front and back yard, and the prettiest flower garden you ever saw. A couple more houses down lived Mr. Dennis. He had a red and white house with a screened-in porch. We used to yell over the fence, "Mr. Dennis, Mr. Dennis" and he would come out with butterscotch candy, peppermints, and the strawberry candy with the green and red wrappers. Oh, and let me not forget the cinnamon candy with the red wrapper. Hmmmmm, some of my best memories.

The picture below is my twin, Bianca, and I with my Aunt Rose. I am on the left. Aunt Rose and Granny were best friends.

Brittney and Bianca with Aunt Rose

2.

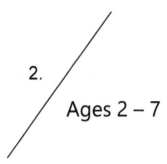

Ages 2 – 7

"Early exposure to trauma, fearful events and high levels of stress affect the developing brain, particularly in the areas involved in emotions and learning."
Early Childhood and Mental Health

PTSD or Post Traumatic Stress Disorder - *"Studies indicate that children can develop PTSD after exposure to a range of traumatic stressors, including violent crime, sexual abuse, natural disasters, and war."*

https://www.ncbi.nlm.nih.gov/pmc/articles/PMC14147 52/

I don't remember much, about being one, two, three, or four. But I do remember my mom being in

Pontiac at a rehab center for her terrible drug addiction. There was a disconnection there. We all have our problems. I came out okay, by the Grace of God.

Brittney left, Bianca right

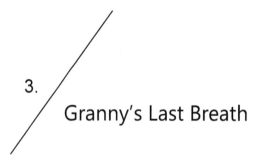

3.

Granny's Last Breath

When I was eight years old my entire life changed. My best friend, the reason I felt the love that I missed from my mom, had gone on to be with the Lord. Granny had died. And I felt like I died right with her. I had never felt such pain at a young age and will never forget that day. I had gone upstairs to see if Granny was still going to take Bae to the doctor. She said "NO, because I'm too sick!" I knew she didn't look like herself. I went on to school, but told her I loved her, and I would see her after school. I wasn't even at school an hour when I got the news.

I was devastated, it was the first time my heart had ever been broken. It was the first time I had ever experienced death, and trauma. But I also wondered what this meant for me? How was I supposed to live without my Granny? Who would make breakfast? Who would fix my wounds? Who would I get into bed with and watch TV with, and eat butterscotch candy with?

I just didn't know how to go on. It took me a while to even talk about her. I buried all the memories I had of her, because it was so painful for me to think about them. Anyway, we went to the hospital and they had moved Granny into a room with a few pieces of equipment, just in case she decided to come back to life. I went in that small room and I talked to my Granny and I needed her to know how much I adored her, and I loved her with everything I had in my 8-year-old heart.

Granny wore a short haircut; she was tall, very slim and brown skinned. She was so well loved, by so many people. I remember the night after the funeral, momma told us not to get ready for bed because we were leaving that night. That is when our adventures started.

Have you seen the movie "The Goonies"? It is a classic movie, about a group of kids who go on an adventure looking for treasure, and they run into some bad guys. They get trapped inside of a building, and they try to outrun the bad guys. They find some things along the way, eventually they find the treasure and all kinds of gold. Yeah, great movie, right? Yeah, that was us. That was me on an adventure, but I never found any treasure, at least not then. Okay, keep reading with me.

We had taken Granny's car, a blue Corsica, and drove to Memphis, Tennessee where we stayed with Aunt Ann and Uncle Frank. I had never been in the country, had never been down south where folks talked funny, and teachers were allowed to whip you in school. A new state meant new drugs and new people for momma, and new adventures for us. After that we bounced around so much, I don't remember where we went after Memphis.

"Life is not about how hard of a hit you can give, it's about how many you can take and still keep moving forward." Rocky Balboa (from the movie Rocky)

My Granny

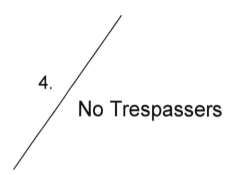

4.
No Trespassers

When I was nine years old, we lived in Kalamazoo, Michigan at the Gospel Mission Shelter. I remember us living there twice on both sides. One side was just a regular shelter where you had a certain amount of time there. The other side was for long-term stay, it was almost like a house. Momma had her room and my sisters and I had our room. The kitchen and everything else, we shared with everyone else. We later had an apartment, but I barely remember any of that.

I remember going to a place called the Drop In, everybody calls it the Soup Kitchen now. Momma met a man named James there. The day she met this man, is the day we stayed over with him and before I knew it, we were living with him. After that the nightmares started, I was living in a real-life horror film. I'm not sure the first time it happened, but it was in the fall. I was raped the entire time I lived in that house. No matter how I tried to hide, he would find me. I was scared and he was desperate, and every single time he found me, whether it was under the bed or in a cabinet, he grabbed me, got on top of me as my insides began to crumble. Yes, I was raped!

Can you imagine a 9-year-old – so young and innocent – wanting nothing to do with life? I died on the inside. I wanted to end my life at that young age. Could anybody see the pain? I guess not, because my granny was gone; the only person who cared.

We were at the park one day and I had to use the restroom. I asked my sisters to come back with me, but they said no. Anyway, I went back, scared for my life. I walked into the house - heart racing, hands sweating, my mind going a mile a minute, because I didn't know what awaited me behind the door. I had used the bathroom and James came in before I pulled my panties up, him: *"Put your leg up on the tub and then I want you to bend over slightly"*, and my dress went up. He penetrated me and I didn't show any emotion. I just froze up as he was moaning and groaning, *"Mmmm, ahhh, that's how I like it"*. If you ask me, I was dead to the world. In my mind, I knew it would be over soon, but days went on and I never said a word. What was a girl to do? I hated my life so much, and I hated everyone in it, because no one could see the heartache and the pain. If they did, it was ignored. Folks see everything else, but they did not see me. Almost like I was invisible, like I didn't exist.

There was a time when we were all in the house and James asked, *"Who wants to help me clean? Brittney, I want you to help me. The rest of y'all go upstairs and don't come back down until I call you."* What kid do you know who likes to clean? That was a dumb question, right? I'm so serious, well – of course I got picked, little ole' Brit. It was James' way of having sex with me. This time we relocated to the kitchen. *"I want you to sit on the table and open your legs".* We heard a loud boom, then James hurried up and pulled out of me, and said, *"Wash those dishes, and you betta not say a word!"* Ugh, just nasty! That pervert knew he was wrong.

I spent most nights hiding under the bed, there weren't many places to hide. Maybe going under the bed gave me a sense of tiny shelter in a small space. No matter where I hid, James found me. *"Brittney, where are you?"* and the repeated game of hide and seek predator vs. prey - continued. This time when James found me, he took me to the back of the room. This time, I'm lying on my back, while this man is moaning and groaning. He used his finger to tear my insides open even more, and forced me to watch pornography, as if what he was doing was not enough.

I remember James asked me once, *"Can you ride with me to pick up my daughter."* But he didn't have a car, so we traveled on a bike. I am riding with him, on a bike, to pick up his daughter and he says, *"Do you want me to stop?"*

I played dumb, *"Uhhhwhatchumean?"* C'mon, who wants to be taken advantage of?

"You know, do you want me to stop?"

Heck yeah I want you to stop! What kind of foolery? I may never understand why this had to be part of my life. But I am thankful that God has strengthened me enough to share my experiences. Keep reading please!

I, being a child, didn't know how to answer. I was just too afraid. Again, where was Kathy, where was the woman that gave birth to me? I didn't know how to respond to James. Now that I am older, I do think my sisters may have known what was going on, it may even have been happening to them and they may have been too afraid to say anything. Now that I think about it, I believe that's why neither of them wanted to come to the house with me that day at the park. I was too afraid to say anything, or he would kill me. I never said a word. Now, you are also probably wondering where my mom was in all of this?

Probably somewhere trying to support her habits. I believed in my heart that she knew what was going on, but made a choice to stay gone. Yep, always missing in action. And she just stayed gone.

Oh well! I am not sure how much longer we lived there. I can't recall if we had gone to a motel or another city, but we stayed in the motel so long that we went to school from there. We would catch the school bus, and when it was time for us to get off the bus, the kids would tease us while laughing *"Y'all live in a motel".* So, we pretended to walk the other way so they wouldn't see us walk into that room. Man! What the heck was wrong with our mom? Why did I have to exist in this world? Wondering when my suffering days would be over? Again, no one saw my pain. And the adventures were just starting.

I do remember leaving to yet another city. I swear we lived all over Michigan. Geez!! If I'm not mistaken, we went to Battle Creek, Michigan and lived in a shelter. We were there long enough to attend school. Bianca and I had a birthday there, I remember because I got the Brandy cd for my birthday. That's all I remember about that.

I didn't like the school we were at because the kids were mean. Momma was all over the place, while her kids were suffering. I didn't know what happened, but momma ended up going to jail, and cousin Rose came to get us from Battle Creek. She took care of us while momma was in jail.

Then we were back in Flint, Michigan. We went past a school that was closed off with police tape. When we asked what happened, we were told that Kayla Rowland was shot and killed by her classmate. I believe she was in the 1st grade. RIP to her.

While we lived with cousin Rose, we started going to Dailey Elementary and I remember we were all at school one day when there was a bomb threat. A boy was picking on me, and I'd had enough. I guess I was just angry, so something in me had enough courage to attack and that's exactly what I did. I beat the boy up and my sisters and I ran home. They never helped me either. Lord, were we ever taught anything? It was a dog eat dog world out there, everybody for themselves.

I guess that was my battle, the kids were so mean there. They talked about me, I was always being made fun of. To them my lips were too big, I was too dark, with big eyes. I don't ever remember being told that I was pretty. Thank God I don't need anyone to tell me that now.

"I praise you, for I am fearfully and wonderfully made. Wonderful are your works; my soul knows it very well." Psalms 139:14

I am fearfully and wonderfully made and so are you. Now smile! I now know WHO I am and WHOSE I am. I love my big brown eyes, my big lips and I love the color of my skin. Black is beautiful! And you reading this, you are beautiful too, no matter what color you are!

I'm not sure how long we stayed with Rose because one night while we were sleeping, momma came "like a thief in the night" and got us. We went to another shelter. From that shelter momma found a house on Bermuda Lane. She told us that we wouldn't have anything in the house, but I guess we were ok with that. I mean, we were used to not having things anyway, so it was nothing new. We moved into this house with no gas, electricity, heat – no nothing. We slept on the floor next to each other, huddled up. The struggle was real. Our food went outside just so it would stay cold. We loved the winter because it was our fridge. No water – we used the neighbor's water hose to do what we needed to do. This was my life, and it wasn't going to change anytime soon.

Months later we started another new school, Buell Elementary where little Kayla had been shot. All the girls there had bad attitudes. I did not have a good elementary school experience. There was a lot of traffic in and out of the house. When Momma was home, she stayed in the bathroom all day. It was her favorite spot. When she left the house, she would be gone all day. I remember so vividly one birthday at that house, momma was gone and all we had was a radio. Sitting on a milk crate, listening to music. We sat in the house that day looking out the window in every direction, wondering when she would walk through the door, and this was how we spent our birthday.

Crack was the most important factor in her life. This is why birthdays are sooo important to me now. If someone remembers my birthday, I believe they care, to a certain extent. She had forgotten about us. We never seemed important to her. Sad thing is we would wait for her to get high and ask if we could go down the street. You see there was food and shelter elsewhere. Anytime I was not with momma, I felt safe.

One night we were all sleep, and I heard someone break in, I pretended to be asleep. Four men in all black clothing, and ski masks unplugged the clock and knocked over the ironing board, looking for something. Momma obviously owed someone money. They took Granny's purse, while looking for it. That's the only memory we had of her. Do you know what she said when the police got there? She thought one of us had fallen out of the bed. Really? We could have been hurt, like she didn't think to get up and check? Let me stop. I thank God for sparing my life. We ended up finding Granny's purse in a field across the street. We also found a dog – frozen, my guess is malnutrition, like us, because when did we really eat?

Well, we ended up getting evicted again, nothing new, that was normal for us, so we went to another shelter in Flint. We went in and all momma had to do was be back at the proper time; she couldn't even do that. We weren't even there for a day before we were put out on the streets; homeless once again. "The Pursuit of Struggle!" Momma called Michael, her first baby daddy. RIP to my big sissy, her name was Brittany Marie Williams. I was named after her. She died when she was a few months old. I guess momma got tired of staying with other people. Geez Louise! About time she got tired. I know I was tired, but hey! That was our lifestyle, so we found ourselves on the road again, not that it was anything new for us. We were used to it.

Brittney was 9 years old in this picture. "I'll never forget because I was wearing Coca Cola lip gloss from CVS.'"

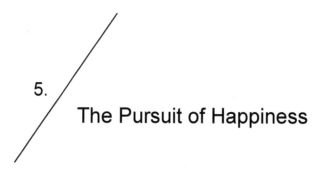

5.

The Pursuit of Happiness

The movie "The Pursuit of Happiness" starring Will Smith and his son Jaden Smith is one of my favorite movies about overcoming the obstacles that life throws at you. Not giving up, no matter how bad things get, but believing in yourself is the one thing that makes life worth living. If you want something bad enough, you will fight for it, you will give everything you can to make sure you come out on top.

Well in my case, we were living in The Pursuit of "Struggle". I didn't have a dream to pursue, nor did I have a suitcase to put it in. We were just another family struggling to get by, living pillar to post. One thing I can say is, we learned to survive, we learned to get by. We struggled so bad I couldn't even afford to think about what I wanted to do when I got older, didn't even think I would make it to see the age of twenty-six. Especially the way my mom was going.

"Everyone thinks we should be happy, because we are young. They don't see the wars that we go through every day." The Freedom Writers

My Pain Runs Deep

Yesterday's pain
Today's rain
My tears have been washed away.
But the heartache remains
Frustration invades
Anger and rage like a hurricane
Destroying any and everything that comes my
way
Don't tell me "it's gonna be ok"
Especially if you never experienced a trial or
two,
Everybody saying "this too shall pass"
But the tribulations just keep on coming
Just when I think I had enough
Life hits me again!
I guess that's the universe's way of making me
tough.
I'm not just telling you what I know

But what I'm going through.
They say what we experience is not for us
But, to encourage someone else

So be encouraged...

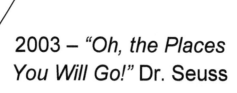

2003 – *"Oh, the Places You Will Go!"* Dr. Seuss

Momma said, *"We are going to Port Huron, Michigan".* We looked at each other and said, *"Port who?"* and laughed. This time it was to an unfamiliar place, hmmm! But this time she was serious. It was a long process, sorry, a long drive. But we made it. Sometimes God has to make us uncomfortable to get our attention, to get us to where we need to be.

Bae, Brandi, Brittney, Bianca – sisters...with Ms. Terry

Breakdown

Boy, this must be serious
Is anybody curious?
Because I have a serious condition
You think I have a drug addiction?
Cocaine, methane
And a little bit of mama, I'm insane
Why did you go down the wrong lane?
It was a one-way
It was so hard to describe
The noise and the unknown voices
It felt like I was in a mental institution
With no solutions
My mind in confusion
Everybody was using
"so" I thought I could do it
But then it caused me to have a mental breakdown

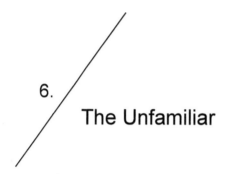

6.

The Unfamiliar

"Welcome to Port Huron, Michigan, boyhood home of Thomas Edison!"

We pull up to a gas station, the Speedway on 24th St., I wanted gum, so I decided to steal it. Momma told me to take it back, wow! That was my favorite gum too – Big Red. Who knew she would care about stealing?

Well, we stayed in a shelter. Momma told the people she had been in an abusive relationship and it worked. Lying always worked for our dysfunctional family, Michael stayed in a men's shelter not too far from where we were. We met Mrs. Thompson there. She was a member at New Hope Tabernacle (now New Covenant Life Ministries International) with Apostle

Nichols. When we started going there, I was 10 years old. I really enjoyed this church because I was able to participate in church activities. I started out in Sunday School. We had some pretty cool youth leaders. Sis. Neisha and Bro. Murphy, everybody was going to New Hope. Well, at least all the kids; we were always having a good time. I started dancing with Ms. Griffin, she was over the youth dance ministry. I always wanted to dance but had no rhythm or coordination. But who needs all that when you are dancing for Jesus? It was a lot of us that were dancing too.

I moved to the choir and was also in the Christmas plays. I was heavily involved in the church and loved every bit of it. It seemed as if my pain was coming to an end. But church was temporary. I had to head home – back to misery.

I started going to Woodrow Wilson Elementary. I loved that school, that's where I went for 5th grade, it's also where I met Tribble. She was my homegirl; we stayed in trouble along with a few other classmates. We were always writing sentences or had lunch detention, almost every day. That's what happens when your parent isn't involved in your life. I wasn't bad, just talked a lot.

We had D.A.R.E. classes, which stood for Drug Abuse Resistance Education. It was a presentation where a police officer came in once a week to teach us about drugs. Here I am learning about drugs, while it's happening in my own home. Officer Brisby was my D.A.R.E. teacher. **Pay attention to the connections,** I've named two people so far. All of this took place during fifth grade. We lived on Military St. at the apartments on the river, then ended up moving to the projects. Those apartments were top of the line. I mean, I'm from Flint and the projects I was used to were raggedy and rundown. Anyway, we ended up moving to Dullhut, everybody referred to this part of town as South Park. We left Woodrow Wilson just before graduation and I was sad about that situation. I had met my best friend there, Maria Boston.

Next, we started going to Cleveland Elementary. I hated that school with a passion. The kids were mean spirited, I was always being talked about. They had way more than I could ever imagine. They had family, they had love, they had food, clothes, and a roof over their head. Half the time we didn't know where we were going to sleep.

The boys were mean and the girls all had their little clicks. I met a friend at Cleveland, her name was Lola Washington – she was my buddy. We lived in the same apartment complex. They were really nice apartments. Everybody knew our family in Dullhut, we were always referred to as "The Twins" because no one could tell Bianca and I apart. We met a lot of people out there. Summers were fun. When it was really hot, they'd have water fights and anybody that walked by got soaked. Even if you were the police, they did not care. I remember we used to take saltine crackers and bologna to the playground and climb up on the jungle gym and eat. This was also when we had the biggest black out, I think the entire state of Michigan experienced this. I'll never forget it because people were talking about how they were stealing from stores. I thought that was funny. The experience was wild. Memories!

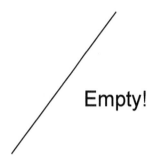

Empty!

Do you know what it's like to come home
To empty cabinets, and an empty fridge,
Especially when your mom is strung out on crack
cocaine,
And can barely tell you her first name.
This is no life anyone should have to live,
But if you can survive
You're good – no worries over here.

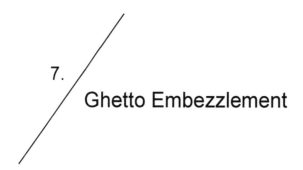

7.

Ghetto Embezzlement

One day when we came home from school, my sister looked into the cabinets - they were empty. She started to cry because we were hungry. There was never food in the house, we had nothing. We were just a ghetto family, looking for a way out. Momma decided to do something about it and began to steal from K-Mart. Clothes and food, that's what we needed, they would go in, grab carts and walk out. "Straight Thuggin!" They were so good that people begin to put in requests for what they wanted, stereos or TV's. If you ask me, they took boostin' to a whole notha' level! Everybody knew what they were doing, it was no longer a secret. They would go and come right back.

I was on the church bus going to Wednesday service and didn't understand any of what was going on. Now that I think about it, it was grace that kept us, because the first time they started stealing they should have been caught. One particular day they had gone, and I knew in my gut that something was wrong, because they didn't come right back. Baejanae stayed back with me; like I said, something was wrong.

Bianca came to me and said, "They bout to take us".
Me: "Who taking us?"
Bianca: "The people."

I looked and saw a bunch of police cars and the Sheriff, so Bae and I ran. We ran to the next apartments, Golden Crest. I was screaming for my life, as if someone was trying to kill me. Someone finally heard my cry and I was able to use their phone. When I called Mrs. Thompson and told her what happened, she came and got us. She ended up driving back to the scene and Momma stopped her. Bae and I were sitting in the back of the car.

It was THE worse day of my stinking life. I cried and cried. No child wants to be taken away from their family, no matter how bad the situation is. At least I didn't.

August 23, 2003, I went into Foster Care. And the day my photo was taken, the one on the cover, it was like I had my own personal mugshot. Anyway, the day I was put in the back of the Child Protective Service car is when I informed them that I had been raped. I recall going to the doctor, being examined and hearing the doctor tell my social worker and foster mom that my vagina had been torn. I'm pretty sure there was more being said, that there was evidence that I had been raped. That was the last I heard about it.

Anyway, back to foster care, this was the summer Bianca and I were so excited about going to Central Middle School. That's where everybody went, the school was hype. What did we know? We were only kids. Well, everybody went there, except me, I never got to go there. I was sent to live with a family out in the country, with Mrs. Jean Ginzel. It was my very first time living with a white family, a lady that probably didn't know how to cook, and do black people hair, nevertheless she had taken us in. The other two were sent back to Port Huron because there was not enough room. We were separated, split up.

We started going to Yale Jr. High, a very un-comfortable place for me. Bianca and I were the only black people there and color mattered at this school. I experienced much hatred and racism because of my skin.

To sum it all up, I just lost my Granny (2000), I was raped (2001), I was homeless (2002) and now I was being taken away from my mom (2003). All in a three-year time span. Now that I think about it, I would probably be on drugs, and on the streets somewhere.

Could things get any worse? Bianca and I had all of our classes together. I guess things begin to loosen up, because the people started to like us. There was a total of five black people in that school. What I hated most about going there was getting up at the crack of dawn to catch the school bus. Lord have mercy! Definitely took some getting used too.

It was a rough time. We eventually got to have visits with the FIA (Family Independence Agency), it's now called DHS (Department of Human Services). Things have changed a lot since I was in the Foster Care system. We started out with supervised visits, then unsupervised, day passes, then overnights. You see it was a process, and I know some of you reading this know that nothing in this life is easy. Everything we do takes time and requires a process. And if you want it bad enough, you will work for it. We were eventually reunited with our mom, she just had to prove herself for three months and she was good to go.

Clearview was the name of the facility where Ms. Mona was in charge. There were curfews, they had to attend Out Patient therapy, go to four or more meetings a week and work or volunteer. They had to attend relapse prevention, meet with the case manager weekly to go over progress, random tests. Hmm, you are probably wondering if she made it? NOPE! Momma snuck her baby daddy in, at least that's what she told us, but we all knew the truth, just someone to get high with. Anyway, Ms. Mona happened to be in the facility when the guy was there. I'll never forget, we were sitting in the kitchen when she came to the patio door and we had to let her in, momma was caught, first violation. Thank God she didn't get kicked out.

Anyway, I was coming from the gym which was in another building, ugh the struggle, and we only had five minutes in between classes. I was coming back from gym and I got a note saying, "Call home as soon as possible". I called, and it was momma, she had gotten into more trouble. She said, *"They already have Brandi and Bae, I'm on my way...don't go anywhere".* Well, she got there at the same time as the cops. But wait, what was she going to do, kidnap us or something? It was so humiliating being taken away from school. Oh well, back to foster care, back to Jean; she really liked us.

I guess I was just tired - fed up, and I began to have tantrums. What was going on in my life? Why was so much happening to me at such a young age? Why was I going through so much? Jean got tired of my tantrums and called to have me removed, but they couldn't remove me without removing my sister. Bianca did not want to leave.

They were going to move us out to Capac,

Michigan; even further away. I slit my wrist, I just didn't want to live anymore. Hoping to die a slow death - I was over all the bull. I hated every bit of my life at 11 years old. I didn't know too much about God, but I never needed him more. I was truly in search of a miracle, getting ready to be moved to my new home.

That same night, I received word that Ms. Griffin (remember, she was the dance minister) was going to get my sisters and I. I was so happy, I felt like God had come through. I got my break, again thank God for GRACE! Ms. Griffin heard that we had gone into foster care, so she got her foster parent license to take us in. We started having those visits again, day passes, supervised at DHS Office, and then unsupervised. Momma even got a house down the street from our foster home, and we would have unsupervised visits there. One particular day we were visiting when Bianca got cold and put on momma's jacket, she put her hand in the pocket and pulled out a small bottle, very small, that had drugs in it, and the 3 of us just looked at each other like a deer in headlights, all I could think was, WHAT NOW?

I knew then that I had a decision to make, do I keep this information to myself, or do I let momma keep trying to fool the system and we end up with her. I made up in my mind that I was going to report this incident to CPS (Child Protective Services). My sisters were very upset with me for what I did. Momma lost her rights April 4, 2004. She didn't fight for us because she knew we were in a good place. At least that's what she said. They asked if our "fathers" wanted us and no one came forward. This was the day I became a ward of the state - the state of Michigan.

Ms. Griffin had 3 girls Tiara, Tiffany, and Diamond. I remember the day she got us, will never forget it. She had told all the family about us. We had gone to Detroit to meet her family. It was a great day. I think, later on, Brandi and Bae came. We had to move to a bigger house, so they could come. We left the North End and moved to Midtown, we stayed on Court St. I thought things were going pretty well and I could let my guard down a little bit. It was time for my sisters to come but, I did not want them there with me. Was I wrong for being a little selfish? I wanted Ms. Griffin to myself. I felt like my sisters and momma had gotten us into this mess.

At that time, I needed someone to tend to my needs and I felt that she could. So much had gone on in my young life. I tried everything I could to get my sisters out of the house. I would tell on my sister as much as I could, each of us considered suicide. Our room was very small with two bunk beds in it, I slept on the bottom bunk. I sat on the floor reading a small book that said Girl Power with young girls of different ages who wrote poems, and as I sat there, I said, "*I can do this, I can write a poem!*" And it's like a light bulb went off in me, I wrote so much! Writing was therapy for me, writing was a form of healing. So much came out of me, you could hear the frustration, the fear and the cries for help in the poetry that I wrote. I had so much to say, and I felt like writing poetry was the best way someone could hear me.

I remember my sister having a belt around her neck, pulling and pulling. Instead of talking to her, I told on her.

Everything she did - I was there so I could tell. Me: "*Ms. Griffin, Brandi has a belt around her neck trying to pull it.*" It didn't work though, I had my own problems. I was never looking for a solution, but was always the one to start problems. The tantrums followed me to Ms. Griffin's house, and after a while she made up her mind she couldn't handle me anymore. I went to the Harbor House, an emergency placement home. I got word that she said I couldn't come back, so I said, "*If she does not want me to go back, then I want to go to another group home*". They found me another foster home.

I stayed with Ms. Woods, she did adult foster care and she had twins, a boy and a girl with Cerebral Palsy. I was there for a few months; didn't last long. The twins ended up going with a relative in Canada. Ms. Woods also had an older man there, he was wheelchair bound and went to the bathroom through a tube which she emptied in the tub. UGH! I was so grossed out that I didn't bathe while I was there. I refused to get in that tub to take a shower. One day she came to me and said I needed to start showering. I looked at her like she was crazy. I did, but I used every cleaning product I could find, including alcohol. I know you are probably thinking, "Ain't nobody got time for that". Ah, the struggle!

I was still going to New Hope Tabernacle and I was a part of SONS (Saving Our Neighborhoods and Streets). Ms. Pearl had been picking me up from the foster home for rehearsals, I danced, sang in the choir, and I stepped. Yep! Didn't think I was any good because of what I was going through. She did and started picking me up at the Harbor House (a facility for youth who are troubled). I was moved to my new foster home, she picked me up and dropped me off there as well. One particular day, I came back about 9 o'clock or later and Ms. Woods decided be upset and get in my face, telling me I was no longer allowed to attend my church, I had to go with her. I was NOT happy about that. As a result, I began to have tantrums. She got rid of me.

On to the next place! I was used to people getting rid of me all the time. I was always being tossed to the side, like some trash.

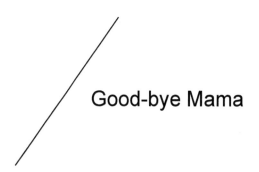

Good-bye Mama

It's hard to believe that I will never be loved the way I want to. I guess I'll have to accept the fact that this is my life. This is the way God wanted it to be. Maybe this is what He planned for me. It hurts to think about my future, since I know you're not in it. I hate that I spend my nights crying, trying to figure out why you gave up.

It's hard to reminisce, especially since I never got a kiss, and I'm pissed because not once did I get a hug. Where was the love? It's hard to remember you being there for me, when I needed you the most. To me, you were just a ghost.

It hurts to think about you, when all I can remember is you, trying to fight a terrible drug addiction, not once did you think about the affliction that you caused me.

I hurt because I don't have love and affection. It's like a fatal attraction, except you're fatal. Oh, I forgot, there was never an attraction. You never tried to make me happy. I hurt because I lack a mother and that is why my life is whack! I hurt because you never tried to get back on the right track. You left and fell in love with crack.

It breaks my heart to know that I don't have a mother, and so I suffer.

It hurts when I'm reminded of you coming in late at night, because you were busy getting your high, but what about you telling me goodnight? Instead I was forced to say....

Goodbye Mama!!

8.

Trashbags (My Suitcase)

On October 27, 2005 I came in from school and my worker told me I was leaving. It was so easy for a foster parent to pick up the phone and call your worker to say he/she does not want you anymore. I had gone to The Children's Home of Detroit, where I would live for a year. I was put into Founders Cottage where I met a lot of girls my age that had been in CHD for quite some time, with stories a lot worse than mine. Some of the girls I still talk to, as well as a few of the staff.

I experienced a lot of unwanted things in this group home although I liked it when I first got there. After a while the place begin to take its toll on me, I wanted out so bad, but I could not leave. I went through a lot of counseling trying to talk about my problems. But the truth is, I was mad as hell. It helped for the moment, there were times when I just wanted to be alone, but there was absolutely no privacy unless you were in the bathroom.

I was so emotional and needy while I was there. After a while I really got used to the place, I became complacent, I got too comfortable and started to blend in with everyone else there. Because I would get put on restriction for having a smart mouth, manipulation, physical aggression, provoking and sometimes bed-time disturbance, I was always in trouble. I always lost my points and was never allowed to go on the Reward Trip at the end of the week. Trying to fit in - that was my problem, wanting to belong to a group of people who were worse off than I was, people who got me into trouble.

Some of the staff were there because they had a job to do. Some of the staff went above and beyond; some even made me feel like I was their child. You generally know who has their heart in something and who are just there for the check. Sad, but that's just the way things go. I got tired of those 7-minute phone calls or those weekend visits. I would call Officer Brisby and we would talk. She always asked me how I was doing at the group home, or if I had gotten into trouble. And I always had to tell the truth, besides she is a police officer and they know when you're lying.

I remember getting into my first fight with a girl who ran her mouth and thought she could run up on me, and thought I was not going to doing anything; yeah right! (I felt so hood, saying that part! Lol.) I was not ok with it. Oh, and I did not get in trouble either. After being at CHD I got tired of being on restriction and learned how to work the system. I was able to do things the other kids could not do. I started going to church with the supervisor of my cottage, Ms. Cherri. But that soon ended, because Ms. Cherri made an announcement that she was resigning and moving. Once again, I felt like I was being abandoned, I felt neglected. She would no longer be working at The Children's Home. I was so hurt by this information. That meant everyone that had become a family in Founders Cottage would be split up among the other cottages - Bewick, Boyer, and Parker Cottage.

Parker Cottage had some of my favorite staff, so I was ok going there, especially because Mrs. Taylor was there, she was my absolute favorite staffer in that group home. But I'll tell you something, if I got mad at one of the staff in Parker, I wanted to leave and go to Bewick. Especially if I didn't get my way and couldn't have what I wanted. I would act a complete fool, and the sad part is, the staff knew when I was putting on, so I would either be put on restriction or I would lose my points. I remember wanting to be adopted by one of the staff there and it almost happened. But God knew what He had planned for my life, and to be honest I do not think I would be where I am today, had that been carried out. Sometimes I think we can abort our own destiny and dreams when we try to rush or do things on our own. Instead of being patient, but at 13 who wants hear that. It makes sense now that I am older.

I remember when the principal wanted me to go to the school on campus first and then attend offsite. I wasn't having that! It' s when I realized I had a voice. I was able to talk to a few people and explain why I wanted to start school on the first day like everybody else. And they listened. I started Grosse Pointe North High School as a freshman.

My first year was ok, I met some amazing people and two girls that were my best friends. They were there for me during a rough period in my life. I met Brittney Pippen and Mytalya (My-tal-ya) Thomas, we were on our way to acting class and got lost in the hallway, the school was so big. We became really good friends. I also met Keisha Bryant (she was doing her thing in the music industry) and I met Patricia Myers, who passed away three days before graduating high school. My heart just broke. I was devastated, she was a bright and beautiful spirit. For the second time in my life, I experienced the tragedy of death.

Then there was a boy that I absolutely adored, his name was R. Jones; he was my boo. I had a big crush on this guy, no one was allowed to like him or even talk to him. I was like Nikki Parker and he was Professor Stanley Oglevee, (from TV show The Parkers) I was such a weird kid in school. Whew! That was my high school sweetie; I wrote him poems and sent him notes for Valentine's Day; St. Patrick's Day. I took care of him, like he was really my man.

School was only eight hours long. At the end of the day, I had to return to the Children's Home and I hated it so much. I was ready to go after a few months. I believe God allows certain situations to bring out the best in us. If we don't experience or go through anything, how can we be an example for someone else who has to travel the same road?

I remember having to learn how to crochet as one of our daily activities. I was so tired of the same routine: wake up, breakfast, chores then get in the van to go to school. After school, staff would pick us up, we had study hour, then outside time, dinner, showers and between all that, talk to the therapist. I really didn't care for her, but I had to talk to her - it was part of my treatment plan. To be honest, I really do not think I would be writing this book now, had it not been for that therapist. I remember telling her I wanted to write a book, I was 13 years old and I'll never forget, she gave me a packet and in the packet it said, "When I was born, When I was one" and so on. I took off from there, and here we are; 13 years later writing this book. I think this is when I realized I could dream, I could see myself doing things that were impossible when I was with momma. Anyway, I learned a great coping skill, we had to take up crochet as a cottage activity, and it was very therapeutic. I still crochet to this day.

I vaguely remember attacking a girl, because she was getting on my nerves. She was sitting on the swing and I just ran up and pushed her. By this time, I was just restless and ready to go. I got a restriction for Physical Aggression, twice. I became weary in what I was doing, not sure how I would reap anything - I really don't know what was wrong with me. Ok yes, I was angry and mad at the world for being in the situation I was in. The circumstances were just too much and I felt like it outweighed any good thing that could have come my way. I DID NOT CARE AT ALL. They could do whatever they wanted to me. But it wasn't going to change who I was. To be honest, WHO WAS I?

I thought I was going to be this way for forever, an unwanted teenager with no friends or family. I thought I was going to be miserable, unappreciated, unwanted and unloved. Again, why did I have to go through this? That was the one question going through my mind constantly. Did anybody care that I was hurting? Especially since my twin and my youngest sister were adopted. I had a lot on my plate. I was certain no one wanted me because I was bad, but how could someone adopt my twin and not me? Talk about no child left behind, I was definitely left behind, and I was not ok with that! I hurt more, I cried more, I was so ready to go, but go where? When was my time going to come? When was anybody going to adopt me? Would I ever have a FOREVER family of my own?

I was scared, frustrated, lonely, depressed. I became furious. I started to get reckless and bored, and I got more and more restrictions. Almost got restrained. I didn't care anymore because I grew tired of waiting; getting my hopes up only to be let down again. I became so anxious that I would go to school and email my social worker and my adoption worker, every single day. I was blessed to have some really amazing social workers Naomi and Michelle. They would be working to find me a home and they did, but I was so stressed out during the process that my hair fell out. It fell out so bad that it was up to my ears, that's how short my hair was.

There was a Caucasian family who wanted me. I would have made their 13th child. I remember going on a home visit with them, they had about seven or eight kids adopted from Africa, and some from the United States. I was so excited someone wanted me, I felt like Charlie when he was searching for the golden ticket on Willy Wonka and the Chocolate Factory, only I never found the ticket. I decided not to go through with the adoption, then it dawned on me, it was too many people there. How on earth were they going to see about me and the needs that I had, the emotional trauma and the drama of not having my momma? Besides, it felt like each kid had part of my personality and I wasn't sure how it would work. SIGH! So, I stayed at The Children's Home a little longer.

When would my dream be realized? When was I going to be able to travel with my suitcase? Without all the baggage? Then I found out that another lady wanted me and I was so excited. Exhale!! Oh, the excitement!

CHILDREN'S HOME OF DETROIT
ADOLESCENT RESTRICTION NOTICE

CHILD'S NAME: Britteny Turner   DATE: 12-14-06

COTTAGE: Parker

ISSUER: TERRI SIMMONS

UNACCEPTABLE BEHAVIOR: MANIPULATING

PRIVILEDGE SUSPENSION (check all that apply):

(X) Loss of Cottage Activities until 12-15-06 BEDTIME

(X) Loss of on-campus activities until 12-15-06 BEDTIME

(X) Loss of off-campus activities until 12-15-06 BEDTIME

(X) Account closed until 12-15-06 BEDTIME

( ) Not able to earn points related to offense during LOA

(X) Will complete one of the following (to be selected by SOD):
    ( ) Write a full letter of apology
    (X) Will write an essay on why this was inappropriate and what better choices could have been made
    ( ) Will complete chores for the peer offended for the LOA period
    ( ) Other: _____

Review Date: By:

Original to Clinical Services for chart
Therapist   CS   Cottage (2 copies)   SOD

Poetry

July 7, 2007

I know you've heard a lot of people say everybody's got a story to tell. You're not the only one. I know how you feel, I've been there, I stood in your shoes (not these shoes). This is my story, my life, my pain, my struggles, my accomplishments, my dreams and my screams.

During my time at The Children's Home, Bianca and I would email each other from school and we communicated through poetry.

What if you could?
What if you could picture me, with you again?
Flash!
Picture this, our family!

57

Can you picture mama?
No!
Daddy, no!
Brother – every day,
Picture another me, in another world.

February 9, 2007

Bianca's (my twin) name was changed to Mya
Only if we could!
Mya, I hope you know
That this is real
Momma let someone else
Deal the cards
Only if we could!
But we do imagine things
To see how it would be
If it was done.
Only if we could
See the things
That's taking our life
And causing hell
Mya, this is the real deal!
So just chill

These were my responses, I was really bummed out
when I couldn't find her response, but we were around
13 or 14 years old. Throughout the book you will find

some poetry, and you will be able to see the growth through the years in what I have to say. I hope you are enjoying this book so far, it has taken me 13 years to write. I got frustrated and cried along the way, I even became discouraged. I pray you will be inspired to speak up about anything that is going on, or that went on in your life. It is never too late to talk to someone.

Here is more poetry. The poems are not in order, I put them where I saw fit.

February 25, 2008

Mama said a lot
But what were the results
Assault.
Crack cocaine.
Shame.
Neglect.
Abuse.
Mama wasn't ready nor prepared
Mama neglected
Four girls and one boy.
Mama didn't
Know what to do.
So, what would you?

February 28, 2008
I remember when I wrote this poem...

Humming til my mama come

When you coming
Cause I need some loving
Is it when I become something
And you put down the crack
Cause you sho' aint sharing
So mama when you coming
I'm just humming a little tune
Waiting on you to finish the song
But I guess I'll keep humming
Until you come home.

April 15, 2008

You said sorry!
But I didn't worry
Because it was only temporary
But you hurried
And I slipped, in misery
Praying that
We'd come home
You said
Sorry over and over
And I continued
To accept your apologies
Because you were my mother.

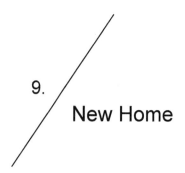

9.
New Home

Who remembers Toy Story 3, when Woody and his gang gets donated to the daycare center? Everything was great when they met Lotso Bear, who gave them the tour of the day care center, and when no one was looking he turned out to be evil, putting Woody and his gang in the worse part of the daycare. It was where the toys got beat up; they got there by mistake. Andy was going to college and Woody had to come up with a plan to rescue himself and his friends. This animated movie was really good. It was not easy, but they managed to get through each obstacle. The Bear ended up going down a totally different road, while Woody and his gang found a home where they were loved on. They felt appreciated, they were so deserving. Well, that's what it was like for me. So here goes.

On July 26th, 2007 I got the word that I was leaving The Children's Home. Some lady wanted me. Finally, I was wanted! She was the sweetest lady you could have ever met. But I was a little on edge about going. I had this fear of meeting a person who would seem nice on the phone but turn into a witch when you got there. And that's exactly what this lady did, she was the worst. I left CHD on July 27th and moved back to Port Huron where I would remain for 3 years. I was with this lady for 3 days. She said some things to me that no child should ever hear. I remember her saying no one wanted me in their home because of my history, because I was bad, and ungrateful; I guess. Just reading a few notes determined the outcome for my life, maybe she thought she was the was the big bad wolf and could tear me down, it didn't happen.

So, I packed my things, which were a Dora the Explorer Backpack and my Journal. She came into the room and said, "*If you leave I'm gonna call the police and have them put you in a detention center!*" This was all because she didn't want to let me attend my church or see my siblings. And so I ran away - I got on out of there. And because I thought I was "bout that life" I kept on going right up to the police myself and asked them if they knew who Officer Brisby was. They said "Yes", then contacted her.

She instructed me to go to her mother-in-law's house until she came and got me. She came and I rode in the back of the police car. That was my first and last time ever riding in the back of a police car. I had never gone to jail, I had never been a criminal, it was exciting and nerve wracking to be sitting in the back of that car. We got to the police station and Officer Brisby called my caseworker. I can remember sitting there scared and feeling unsure because I did not know what the outcome would be, what was gonna happen? Where would I go? Who would be my new family? I remember hearing countless stories of children being released from group homes, they run away and end up right back where they started. I just didn't want to be one of those statistics. And I remember begging Officer Brisby to let me come and live with her.

I was sitting at her desk, we were talking about what went on, and why I did what I did. To sum it all up, the lady said some stuff I didn't like and here we are sitting at the police station. She kept saying, "*Brittney I have rules*". My response, "*I know*", and she was not lying when she said she had rules.

10.
Law and Order

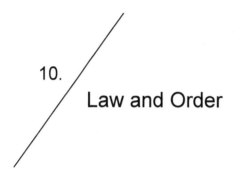

"This is not a Democracy, this is a Dictatorship!"
Bobby Brisby

In other words, *"You don't run SQUAT!"* I moved in with Officer Brisby on August 1, 2007 and I remained there until I graduated high school. It was the longest time in a foster home I had ever been in, and it was the best. Now, I would be lying if I told you it was a perfect home. I acted out on several occasions, had tantrums, lost my cool and many times my foster parents wanted to give me back. But through it all they held onto me. They loved me through my pain and what I was going through. *"The race is not given to the swift nor the battle to the strong, nor bread to the wise, nor richest to the intelligent, nor favor to those with knowledge,*

65

but time and chance happen to them all."
Ecclesiastes 9:11

And let me tell you, these people ENDURED to the end, they fought a beautiful fight, never gave in to any of my tactics, my manipulations, my pity, my bad behavior, but they became a strong couple. I felt as though they nurtured me during my stay there, they took care of someone else's child because my mom was incapable. These are my parents, no doubt about that, no matter where I go, I know that they are there for me; no matter what I do. That's unconditional, and that's what I was looking for.

They had 2 daughters and 1 granddaughter, so for me that meant I was getting 2 big sisters. One sister sometimes got me out of trouble if I was on punishment. I used to text her and have her get me to stay the night at her house so I could leave home. It worked sometimes, then there was a time I had a cell phone. It seemed like it took me forever to get, but I decided to make a FB post and it was on Father's Day. My status said "It's just another day", and I got in trouble because my foster sister told on me. I got my phone taken, and thought I would delete all text messages and put a password on it. But my foster dad asked for it. Ugh, I could not get away with anything.

My other foster sister Amber was a little tougher, she didn't get on my nerves but I felt like she was never on my side. She didn't stick up for me, she never helped me get off punishment, but I did love it when she came home. And I enjoyed talking to her. At first, I thought she didn't like me, or she thought I was this weird little girl, but I enjoyed our moments together. They were always special to me, even now when I call her, I cherish the time I have with my sister. Now, she will tell me like it is, no sugar coating, but I guess that's what big sisters are for.

I was a very angry teenager, I harbored anger in my heart, and hatred. Mad at the world, pretty much mad at everybody and constantly asking why my mom gave me up, why didn't she fight? Why didn't she stay clean? I constantly longed for love from a mother, even at 25 I still yearned for a mother's love. I had my moments though; some days more than you could think. My first year living with the Brisby's was my best year.

I went to Port Huron High School. It was another road block for me because both my foster sisters went to the same school and I had some of the teachers they had. I wasn't getting away with anything! Besides when your foster parents are the police, what can you get away with? I remember coming home crying and just lying in bed. I sobbed and I sobbed because I felt ugly, I felt unworthy, I felt dirty, never felt pretty, and I remember crying up in my room. My foster parents came into my room to see what was wrong, I had never felt so loved by two people at the same time. I knew then that they cared about me. This wasn't just some place for me to sleep and go to school, but I was going to grow there, I was going to excel. I knew I was safe. I got involved in a lot of activities inside and outside of church. I was on the dance team at school, which I hated because we never won an award, and at church I was even on color guard, which I got tired of.

One of the things about the Brisby's, once you got involved in something there was no quitting. And I had never finished anything that I started. I go to a foster home and I leave. I go to another, and I just kept repeating that cycle. Now I had to finish what I started. So, I thought I would get myself kicked off since I couldn't quit. I thought I was doing something, but they peeped my game, and I was on punishment the rest of the school year. I was good at manipulating, so I thought, but they weren't having it, especially with them being cops. I stayed on punishment, always into something. I never did what I was supposed to do, I had a smart mouth and was just trying to do what I wanted to do.

They were the first ones to ever care about my grades. I came home with a horrible report card and the first time they saw my grades - they were not having it. After that first threat, I decided to get my grades together. I didn't want any whippings and I didn't want to be on punishment, so I worked my butt off. When I moved into the house, my Grade Point

Average was 1.7 and when I left them, I had a 3.0. This is what a two-parent household was all about, two parents who loved me and wanted to see me thrive in life.

I wasn't going to just get through life, they had invested so much of their time, and poured so much love into me. They taught me discipline, morals and values that are still with me today. I even had chores, and I had to get them done before I could go to the mall on Friday. I got an allowance and I had to be in the bed at 9pm. I hated that, none of my friends had a bedtime, but Officer Brisby was clear. She wasn't nobody else's momma, and they weren't in her house.

And, you'd better believe you were going to church, you were going to be involved, either you were going to usher or be in the choir. Oh, and if you weren't in the car by the time she was ready to go, you were getting left which automatically meant you were on punishment. I guess I had finally found the 'perfect' home. I had met my match. So, so glad they didn't give up on me. As bad as they wanted to pick up the phone and call my social worker, they didn't. They truly fought the fight, they finished the race.

While I was with the Brisby's I was told that I was getting a new social worker. I had grown to love Naomi and Michelle especially since they had worked so hard to get me out of the group home and they had been with me since I was with Jean in my first foster home. I wasn't sure about having to adjust and talk to someone new. I just wasn't having it.

Social Worker: "Hi I'm Heather, I'm going to be your new social worker."
Me: "I don't need a new social worker, I'm good with the one I have."

Clearly you all can see I am not good with transition, I don't like change. Why are you coming up in here trying to take over, is what I'm thinking. I don't need this lady. Ms. Heather came into my life in 2008 shortly after I had been with the Brisby's and I still wasn't feeling her. You see, it took time for me to get used to new people, had to make sure they weren't out to get me.

The People of the State of Michigan v. James December 22, 2008

Also, during my stay with the Brisby's, I had a visit from some detectives regarding the rape case I had made a few years prior. I thought they had forgotten about me, but I was ok because I had gone through years of therapy and talked about the rape in group therapy. Spent years getting it out of my system. I was in a great foster home and had great parents, so I was doing pretty good. I was 16 years old, a sophomore in high school. Why on earth did it take so long? It took them eight years to come back with a case. By this time, I was a thug. Nothing was going to stop me or get in my way. I spoke to two detectives, one was male and the other was female. They were dressed in all black, almost like a scene from the movie, Men in Black. They asked several questions like:

Lady: *"When was the first time James touched you? How did James touch you? Did he use his body part? What body part was used?"*
Then they showed pictures.
Me: *"I remember this room, there were 2 beds and then walk in the back and there was another bed, and so on."*
Lady: *"Are you familiar with this room?"*
Me: *"I've never seen that room before."*
Then to my surprise, and this blew me away, I saw my twin there as well.
Me: *"What are you doing here?"*
Twin: *"It happened to me too!"*

I was speechless, I could not believe this monster had done the same thing to my sister. I had no idea at the time! That explains why certain things, like the room in the picture, I did not know about but when they showed her, she knew what it was. I never knew the monster had a room, I always saw him and momma sleeping on the pullout couch. Man, my twin had kept it a secret for so many years.

We had been subpoenaed to court which was so hard, having to talk about what happened in detail. My sister and I would laugh and make jokes. I used to cringe when I heard the word penis or vagina.

Twin: *I'm not gone cry when I go up on the stand.*
Me: *I'm not gone cry, because I'm a thug!*

The trial took nearly a week to complete, and through this experience I had parents to comfort me. The support they showed me was surreal, it made me feel like I was the most important person in their life. I actually mattered to someone, I wasn't just a child with a suitcase and a dream. If ever I was in public and saw a strange man while I was alone, I instantly got paranoid because I thought someone was going to attack me. I felt that way for a long time, but now that James was in the picture, that fear intensified. Even now, my worst fear is being raped at age 26 and being helpless. I was scared of the dark and refused to sleep with a closet open because I felt like someone was in there and they were watching me. For a very long time, I slept with my head covered. I had to turn on a light to go to the bathroom, truly the dark gave me goose bumps, it scared the mess out of me.

I lived this life for quite a while until I realized that the monster who had taken away my innocence, would remain behind bars for 35-60 years on four counts of Criminal Sexual Conduct. My twin and I had put a serial rapist behind bars! Eight years later, James was behind bars! I was finally able to unpack some things that I had been traveling with for such a long time. Still carrying the thoughts of being abandoned and neglected with me. Traveling with unnecessary baggage can weigh a person down and that's what it did to me. When I got to the Brisby's house, I had so much baggage - mentally and physically - that it took time to throw stuff out. I kept seeing a therapist to help me with the things I had been struggling with.

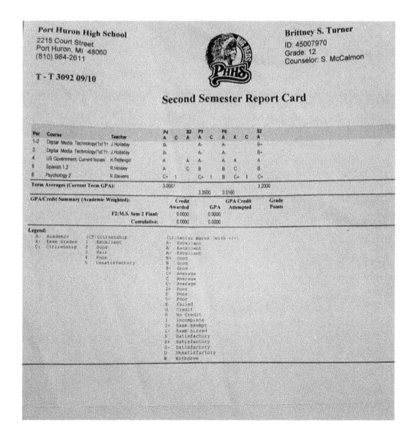

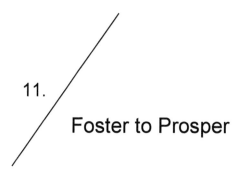

11.

Foster to Prosper

I also served on the St. Clair County Youth Board, called V.O.Y.S.S. (Voices of Youth Standing Strong). It was a group of adopted and foster kids that came together once a month to discuss the Foster Care System and how we can help change it. A few of us were selected to speak at training sessions for new foster parents. Some of us attended conferences to represent the board. I served as the Historian for two years and the President for one year.

We wrote letters to the State of Michigan. There was so much going on in the foster care system that only we, in VOYSS, could be a voice for. Any issue, or anything we did not agree with, we were able to discuss and come up with ways to make it better starting with the county I was in. Being on this youth board made me feel empowered, it made me feel like I had a sense of control over what went on in my life. I attended a conference at Central Michigan University called "Rising Above the Odds". That is where I met Cherish Thomas. I love that woman to the moon and back, literally! Talk about someone who beat the system. And she is still doing it. She has made a big difference in the lives of so many young people, including me. There were a lot of opportunities for us foster children, like having the opportunity to attend college, learning how to balance a check book, how to budget, how to sort clothes for laundry, how to sew on a button. Just basic life skills that some of us did not learn because our parents were incapable. These things were not even thought of before the system got involved, not by foster kids or foster parents. So yes, I am grateful for my foster care experience and the things that it taught me.

I believe that God has to 'disconnect' some things in our lives in order to reconnect. I used to tell people *" You lose a lot coming in, but you gain so much more going out."* Yes, it hurts, but what feels good? In the end, the reward is so much better.

Now that I think about it, God has been there all along, when I didn't think he was present, he was working on my behalf. We get so focused on the things that happen to us, rather than looking at the big picture. I don't get upset anymore because of what happened to me, but I thank God that I was not strung out on drugs, that I did not become a prostitute, and I am grateful that I did not let the system break me. For those of you reading this who may currently be in the foster care system, incarcerated, or you may be feeling hopeless, I want you to be encouraged.

"Have not I commanded thee? Be strong and of a good courage; be not afraid, neither be thou dismayed: for the Lord thy God is with thee whithersoever thou goest." Joshua 1:9

Foster care had its ups and its downs. There were things I wanted to do, but wasn't allowed to because I was a ward of the court.

I had to have permission to leave the state of Michigan. It was depressing at times. When it came time to visit colleges out of state, I was not able to go because it was last minute and I did not have permission. However, I did go on a family trip with my foster parents. We went to a wedding in Mississippi and had gone to New Orleans. We went to Disney World in Florida. That trip to Florida is when I lost my mind. I cut up so bad that my foster dad was ready to send me back. When I got mad at my foster mom, I took my anger and frustrations out on my foster dad. I think because I so desperately wanted a mom, I wanted her to be more than what she was offering me, I wanted her to love me like she loved her own girls.

I am so grateful that my foster parents never threw in the towel when I spazzed out or had a temper tantrum because I couldn't get my way. Their tough love and strict rules helped to cultivate me into the young woman that I am today. A year went on and I was still a part of the Brisby family. Even though I was hurting, they were still patient with me. It was a learning experience for all of us. I have a relationship with them to this very day. Even through all of that, I found myself asking them to adopt me, because I had been with them for so long.

Officer Brisby, my foster mom: *"Brittney you don't have to be adopted to be part of a family, you are a part of THIS family."*

Those words stuck with me for a long time, I am part of the Brisby family, guys, I am part of a family!

Let's not forget that I was always on punishment. I got tired of that too, and couldn't wait to turn 18 and graduate because my foster mom wouldn't let me do anything. I know I'm not the only one who was ready to leave home because their parents were strict. And now you wish you could go back!

I patiently waited for graduation to come. My twin

and I would be the first to graduate in our family. They allowed us to walk together even though she had been adopted, which I thought was pretty cool. Part of me was anxious to get out into the real world as a young adult. Not the world that landed me in Foster Care and a group home, but the world that offered me a new sense of hope and a different path. Throughout the years, I had gotten rid of baggage and at 18, I had a new suitcase. It was not beat up, it was not over-packed and it wasn't over weight. It didn't cost a fee to carry, so I was pretty good with the way things turned out for me. I had graduated high school and it was time to start my new life, as a young adult.

12.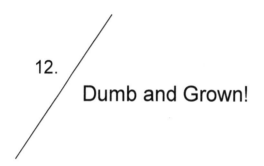

Dumb and Grown!

I had gone to Rochester College, it was a small Christian College in Rochester Hills, Michigan. I spent some time in Flint trying to mend a broken relationship with my mother, when I should've been in school. But I didn't know any better. No one told me, I was just out there on my own. I knew nothing about transitioning; probably because I didn't care when I was in the system. I didn't care about budgeting or transition, everything they taught, I pretty much said forget it. I was over the system.

I was so anxious and READY. I failed every class. I even tried to end my life on several occasions. What was the point of living? Alcohol had become my very best friend. I used to sit in the dorm drinking Four Loko until I didn't know where I was. I tried taking pills, rubbing alcohol, and Nyquil. I was so over life, but my life was saved one day.

Arie, my friend, had come to the room, just before I got ready to take the rubbing alcohol. She called the ambulance and I was rushed to the hospital. My foster parents were there, as well as my mentor. And I was later sent to a hospital for an evaluation. To my surprise there was nothing wrong with me other than I was depressed in a world so big. How could one be so lonely? I was lost; all I wanted was to be loved. And like I said, I found it all in the wrong things.

I was going to counseling, but was not benefiting from it. I was just another statistic aging out of foster care. I was going be just like the other people who came before me. Who cared about me? No one! I may have not carried that big suitcase, but I definitely had a carry-on, because I constantly thought no one cared about me. When things went sour, I was all over the place. Nobody could tell me nothing. I didn't have any parents, nobody could tell me what to do. I remember searching, just searching for love any and everywhere. Whether it was through alcohol or through sex, I had to fulfill the need to be wanted by any means necessary - male or female. I found myself sleeping with random guys in an abandoned apartment on a dirty mattress. I thought, since I was abandoned, it was ok for me to be there, right?

I found myself with a guy twice my age in a halfway house, with my suitcase. This guy had been on a tether. I didn't even know why he was on it and I was barely eighteen. I met this grown man at the church, and I can remember feeling so desperate and vulnerable that I called him up. The sad part is, I don't even remember his name. He answered.

Him: *"HELLO!"*
Me: *"This is Brittney from church, I need somewhere to stay."*
Him: *"You can come stay here, with me."*

I just knew I needed a place to stay. Me and my lil' suitcase went to his house. He gave me his room while he slept downstairs on the couch, then he would cook breakfast, lunch, and dinner. It was like I was his 'sweet' lady. My man was on a tether. We weren't having sex, but I felt that was coming next. So, when I heard he was getting off the tether, me and my suitcase went on to the next destination, wherever that was. I found myself dipping into things that probably should've left me with STD'S and other things. I found myself having a girlfriend, secretly, no one knew about this.

It was a hustle and flow mentality for me. I had to get what I needed and keep going. I wouldn't allow myself to think about anything I was doing, that meant I would be caught up in my emotions and I just didn't have time to think about the things I was doing. My girlfriend came through for me when I needed her - she was my drug and I was feigning for her like Jodeci. She was my supplier, she supplied me with artificial love. But I could never get the high I intended, so I went back to sleeping with strangers, putting my own life in danger, sexting and texting. Skyping with folks that weren't even my type, trying to keep up with the hype.

And if I got pregnant it wasn't no faking it. But I had a plan all figured out in my head, I couldn't have a baby so I wanted it dead. I drank one day until it came out in the toilet, flushed it and went on with my life. Never told a soul, I thought I would grow old and take it to my grave, and then I decided to write a book!

I know it would have a lot of y'all shook, but I had to tell the truth since that's the only way to be free, right? I was really scared of unpacking my suitcase, because I didn't know what other travelers would think about me and my dirty laundry. I thought I could unpack the little stuff. I started traveling with this book in my head when I was 13 ... never thought I would actually write it for the world to see.

Sex for a Bed!

Learning to love
But not what's between your legs,
I don't want to be the one to beg
And seem desperate for a simple piece of ass
Knowing it probably wouldn't last but a second.
See I used to creep because I needed a place
to sleep
Sex for a bed in exchange for some head, and I
didn't even
Get breakfast in bed.
Sorry boo, you were just a midnight rendezvous
I'm pretty sure you had no clue
but my body just wanted you.
It's a hustle and flow mentality
You gotta get it where you can.
I'm just saying you were never
supposed to be my man.

And that was how I lived my 18-year-old life. What else was there to do? Being on my own and out of the Brisby's house, I once again felt abandoned. I got a secret girlfriend on standby. But I couldn't let anyone know about her, they might think something about me. Besides I was for Jesus in my public life, I was really screwed up! I cared so much about people and their opinions that I'd do whatever I needed to do, to make sure they stayed in my life. I was a people pleaser. For so long people would come into my life and then leave. I wanted them to stay.

That's the way life was, nobody was permanent, so I begin to treat my relationships that way. I would do the hurting and the abandonment. Let me get them first, before they got me. Still angry and hurt, not knowing who I was or what it was that I was supposed to be doing, I went my own way. Down my own path of self-destruction. Again, who really cared about Brittney and what she was going through? I didn't and neither did anyone else. The pain began to be too much to bear. I wanted out, but if I got out - where would I go?

Who would help me? I was still enrolled at Rochester College but later stopped going to classes and just lived there. I just existed and I did that for two years straight. I had a few people in my corner who appeared to care; at least I think they did. Ms. Bryan, Mrs. Courtney and Mrs. Schaffer, these women meant business. I could not do what I wanted to do, these people actually cared about me and what I did with my life. They were strict and there was no manipulating allowed. Besides, the three of them knew each other. I guess they weren't about to play any games with me. I would skip class and go sit right under Mrs. Schaffer or on the floor and we would talk about life. As you can see, I hated mine and almost everything that had ever happened. There were times Mrs. Schaffer would take me to basketball games. I'll never forget when we went to the Pistons games, they were playing the Lakers and I met Shannon Brown, who is now married to the singer Monica. I thought that was the happiest day of my life. And pretty cool at the same time.

During my time at Rochester College, Mrs. Schaffer became the mother I had been longing for, for so long; even though it was temporary. She was what I needed in my life, I was fresh out of the system, trying to figure life out. I had a few moments where I thought I was grown.

Like the lil hoopty I had. Me and my two home girls decided to go joyriding. My Mercury Cougar decided to break down. Everybody's phones were about to die. I could only call Mrs. Schaffer and when she came to get us, she cussed me out from Detroit to Chicago. It was almost like if you made the wrong move, your life was going to flash before your eyes. I still laugh at this. One of the sweetest ladies ever, blew a fuse because I decided to be dumb and grown, and I still talk to her to this day. She has loved me and never stopped.

There was not one person who knew pain like I did. At least that's how I felt. It was pretty scary being out there. I just wanted my family - not a foster family - just my own biological family. I felt empty even though I'd had the Brisbys. I still felt a void, I still felt incomplete.

13.

Traveling Light

Whenever we travel, we tend to over pack, making the suitcase over weight. Now you are forced to take some stuff out (fear, abandonment, neglect, hurt, etc.) or pay the baggage fee, and believe me it is not cheap. I have learned over the years to always travel light, because I'm always going go shopping (peace of mind, self-love, wisdom) and these are some of the best gifts you could ever have.

What unnecessary things are you traveling with? Write them down so you can see them:

_____

_____

_____

_____

_____

_____

_____

_____

_____

_____

_____

_____

_____

_____

_____

_____

_____

_____

_____

_____

_____

A Depressed Mess

I need someone to rid my mind
Of these thoughts
I keep getting caught
Thoughts of suicide surround my head
Like a dead creature, covered with flies
These thoughts are eating me alive
Feel like I'm gonna have a meltdown
Lord, I desperately need a sign
I wanna run and cry,
Because my mind
Is going a mile a minute
I can't think and I can't blink
My thoughts are weak
And my tears leak
Like a never-ending creek
I'm drowning in negativity
I can't reach my happy place
It has gone to outer space

And I've become a disgrace
To my own face
I can't keep up with the pace
Because my thoughts have been laced
With suicide
And I don't even like that side!
Now I lack pride
And I struggle to survive
Lord, this is my cry
As you can see, I tried.

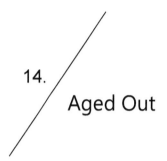

14.

Aged Out

My life has not been a walk in the park. The road has not been easy, but I wouldn't trade my heartache, my pain for nothing in this world. I believe it has made me a stronger woman because of it, I have become more independent, I am confident and more developed in dealing with life. I thank God for giving me the strength to endure the things that I had to go through.

"There is no greater agony than bearing an untold story." Maya Angelou

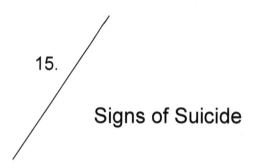

15.

Signs of Suicide

- o Talking about wanting to die or to kill oneself
- o Looking for a way to kill oneself
- o Talking about feeling hopeless or having no reason to live
- o Talking about feeling trapped or in unbearable pain
- o Talking about being a burden to others
- o Increasing the use of alcohol or drugs
- o Acting anxious or agitated; behaving recklessly
- o Sleeping too little or too much
- o Withdrawing or feeling isolated
- o Showing rage or talking about seeking revenge
- o Displaying extreme mood swings

National Suicide Prevention Lifeline 1-800-273-8255

Additional resources. Currently in 2019, 24 states that will allow aged out youth (18 to 25 years old in most states) to receive Medicaid. please be vigilant in getting the support you need, it's there! These are those states: Alabama

- Arkansas

- California
- Connecticut
- Washington, DC
- Hawaii
- Illinois
- Indiana
- Maine
- Maryland
- Michigan
- Massachusetts
- Minnesota
- Nebraska
- New York
- North Dakota
- Oregon
- Pennsylvania
- Tennessee
- Texas
- Virginia
- Washington
- West Virginia
- Wisconsin
- Pascua Yaqui, AZ
- Eastern Band of Cherokee, NC
- Navajo Nation
- Keweenaw Bay Indian Community
- Tolowa Dee-ni' Nation

For further assistance email
suitcasedreamfostercare@gmail.com

Memories

Baby Brittney

Brittney & Bianca

cousins

Brittney, Brandi & Bianca

8th Grade   6th grade   7th grade

The twins speaking at foster care event

Brittney & Bianca

Brittney, Bianca & Brandi

foster care summer event

Jean Ginzel and family

Ms Griffin & family

With Officer Brisby at Disneyworld

The Brisbys

The Brisby's visiting Brittney in Georgia

Bianca, Bae, Eddie Brittney

Bae, Brandi, Kathy, Brittney, Eddie, Bianca
after 16 years

With the Brisby's at the Mississippi wedding

The Group Home

Memories

Brittney in High School

Brittney and foster sister Amber

Brittney & Bianca at prom with principal

Brittney and Kayla

Britttney and Joi

Brittney with Mrs Jll, therapist

Author

Brittney Sherell grew up in the foster care system and because of PTSD from her childhood, she has been diagnosed with major depression, excessive anxiety, bipolar disorder and borderline personality disorder. As she has gone through treatment, she realizes the importance of mental health treatment.

Brittney is now a foster care warrior, and a poet. She writes to encourage others to be the best that they can be. Her hope is that understanding who she is and how the foster care system works, others will be uplifted, inspired and empowered; never afraid to ask for help. Every voice should be heard!

You may contact Brittney for speaking engagements, book discussions, etc.:
Email: suitcasedreamfostercare@gmail.com
Instagram: @poeticvoice1992
Facebook: Brittney Sherell Turner
Twitter: @poeticvoice1992

New books coming soon!

CPSIA information can be obtained
at www.ICGtesting.com
Printed in the USA
BVHW022205050622
638958BV00013B/46